No Wound Too Deep
For the Deep
Love of Christ

Lisa Buffaloe

No Wound Too Deep For The Deep Love Of Christ
© 2014 Lisa Buffaloe (updated 07/23/23)

Published by John 15:11 Publications, Florence, AL

Scripture taken from the English Standard Version (ESV) The Holy Bible, English Standard Version Copyright © 2001 by Crossway Bibles, a division of Good News Publishers.

Scripture taken from the New Century Version® (NCV). Copyright © 2005 by Thomas Nelson, Inc. Used by permission. All rights reserved.

Scripture taken from the NEW AMERICAN STANDARD BIBLE® (NASB), Copyright © 1960, 1962, 1963 ,1968, 1971, 1972, 1973 ,1975, 1977, 1995 by The Lockman Foundation. Used by permission.

Scripture quotations marked (NLT) are taken from the Holy Bible, New Living Translation, copyright © 1996, 2004, 2007 by Tyndale House Foundation. Used by permission of Tyndale House Publishers, Inc., Carol Stream, Illinois 60188. All rights reserved.

THE HOLY BIBLE, NEW INTERNATIONAL VERSION®, NIV® Copyright © 1973, 1978, 1984, 2011 by Biblica, Inc.™ Used by permission. All rights reserved worldwide.

Scripture taken from the New King James Version®. Copyright © 1982 by Thomas Nelson, Inc. Used by permission. All rights reserved.

Scripture taken from *The Message*. Copyright © 1993, 1994, 1995, 1996, 2000, 2001, 2002. Used by permission of NavPress Publishing Group.

Scripture quotations marked HCSB are taken from the Holman Christian Standard Bible®, Copyright © 1999, 2000, 2002, 2003, 2009 by Holman Bible Publishers. Used by permission.

Holman Christian Standard Bible®, Holman CSB®, and HCSB® are federally registered trademarks of Holman Bible Publishers.

Scripture marked ERV, Copyright ©2006 World Bible Translation Center.

Cover photo by Lisa Buffaloe.
Cover graphics and design by Scott Buffaloe.

ASIN: B00GFZYIP2
ISBN: 9780985929596
ISBN: 9780692206874

Table of Contents

Wounded

I'm so sorry for your wounds. So very sorry for what life has done to you. My heart aches for you. I don't have a magic potion, or enough hugs, or love enough to fix anyone's problems, but I do know a loving, healing, restoring God. And I know what He does with broken, messed up, wounded lives. I've seen how God has restored my life, those I know, and those I'm blessed to interview on Living Joyfully Free Radio. I've personally seen what God has done in the past and what He is doing today.

I understand wounds. I was raised in a Christian home by parents who loved one another and loved the Lord. However, no one knew (including my parents) what was happening behind the scenes. I was molested by a baby-sitter, assaulted by two guys in high school, chased by a man with a knife in a parking lot, had a shotgun pointed at me as two men tried to run me off the road, and I've been raped by a doctor. I've been drugged and locked up, divorced, stalked, had cancer, and experienced the loss of family and friends to death. I've had multiple surgeries and over eleven years of chronic illness from Lyme Disease.

I've made mistakes and had many failures. I've needed to forgive others and forgive myself.

I have wounds inside and out, scars from falls and bumps and bruises of life. Scars from surgeon knives, and scars from the self-inflicted attempts to rid the hurt inside.

However, the more trials I have endured, the more I see God's unending faithfulness and love. Each wound, every soul-scar brought to God for healing has given greater understanding of the depth and width of God's love.

God's gentle touch and unfailing love restores and transforms everything the enemy meant for evil to turn it into good.

I am not a professional counselor and do not have all the answers. Please know counselors are a blessing. The medical community is a blessing. Reaching out for help is a blessing given by God. Please don't hesitate to contact doctors or counselors when needed.

The steps in this book are merely ones I've found helpful in my journey to healing from past hurts.

Jesus's love is deep and flows free to those who are wounded.

Beyond Self-Medication

Wounds exist from negative words pronounced over us by others, evil actions, or even our own mistakes. Many try to use bandages of good thoughts, ignoring the past, or pulling up the bootstraps, or becoming bitter negative people trapped in the victim mode. Self-medication never works.

Soul-scars run so very deep. Inside wounds cause a desperate search for a solution to rid the nightmares and memories.

The past hurts, the enemy taunts, and hidden areas in life only fester in the darkness. Some are like burrs in socks, constantly annoying and pricking with pain, while others are open, gashing wounds.

The enemy wants you to believe your wounds are incurable and your past is unredeemable; that your pain, your sin, and your experiences are too far from God's healing touch. Then Satan fuels the attacks, by trying to keep you quiet and live in shame.

Satan can't beat God, so he uses relentless attacks, attempting to destroy God's creations and the objects of His affections.

The enemy, like a sleight-of-hand magician, wants to redirect our focus, to only see the evil, the bad in others, the hopelessness and futility.

The devil is out to spoil anything good by planting doubts, insecurities, lies, and stirring the pots of the past to create havoc and destruction.

Isn't it interesting how Satan deflects the very evil he created by planting the question, "How could God do such a thing?" And humanity bites the lie--hook, line, and sinker. We forget to point the finger at the one who is causing all the trouble in the first place.

The enemy knows our hidden wounds since he was the instigator. He uses past hurts to question God's goodness, and our worth as a person, as well as to isolate us from others and from God.

The last thing the enemy wants is our freedom, and he works hard to convince us we should keep some things hidden and locked away.

For years I hid my past. I believed the enemy's lies that no one needed to know, and because of the bad things done to me, I would be unlovable.

God provided healing by gently peeling back every layer, then covering each sin and each negative memory with His truth. Through His grace and loving touch came restoration.

When I first went public with my experiences, I cannot tell you how many women sent me messages, or stopped me at church, to share they also had things hidden.

No matter who you are, what you've done, or what has been done to you, God has provided the opportunity for a new life, and He is always faithful to finish what He starts.

We don't have to limp through life. We don't have to believe the enemy's lies that some things are just too bad or too deep for God's healing touch.

St. Augustine wrote, "In my deepest wound I saw Your glory, and it dazzled me."

I love that quote, because in our deep wounds we find the deep love of Christ.

Peace, comfort, and healing comes through The One who is peace, comfort, and healing. Soul-healing comes through Jesus Christ.

We don't muster up our own healing. It is in submitting to Christ, resting in His sovereignty, power, and skills to recreate and renew.

The past cannot be erased, we can't change or erase any of it, we can't control today or the future, but we can take every bit to the Great Physician – God.

I have a friend who is a wound nurse. Her job is to help bring healing to those with deep wounds. And I do mean deep wounds. Some of what she shared applies to soul-wounds.

I'm not an expert, I don't have all the answers, but I do know God is available for every need. The following pages contain steps that I pray will help in the healing of your internal wounds.

Step 1 - Call For Help

God is The Great Physician. There is no one more qualified, no one more loving, no one more skilled, and no one else who has your complete best interest at heart. Keep in mind that He knows the complete picture from now until eternity. Run to His shelter and call 911.

Psalm 91:1 reminds us, "He who dwells in the shelter of the Most High will abide in the shadow of the Almighty."

It is in God's presence we find the answers, the healing, the renewal, the ability to forgive, the escape from the nightmares and memories. It is in God, in the knowledge that He will do what is right, that He is just and righteous. It is in trusting, believing, knowing God and His word. Knowing His heart, especially when we don't understand and when life is so very hard.

It is in knowing God we find all we need. It is in listening to the voice of truth above the enemy's lies. It is knowing The Truth, which is Jesus.

It is in knowing God's word, because when we read His word we see the truth of what happened to those who suffered and the good that came from that suffering. It is in knowing God and surrendering to God. Regardless of what our eyes see and what we have experienced, it is in knowing that God will do what is right, that justice WILL be served, and that He truly does take what the enemy meant for evil and turn it into good.

It is in surrendering to God that we process through the process of our healing.

I've been blessed to interview people on Living Joyfully Free Radio, and person after person testifies to what God has done in their lives, the healing they have received, regardless of how bad the experience. No matter how horrific the past, God's healing was there for each of them. And that healing is also available for you.

Please understand and know that God is love. He is Love, not the emotion. God is love, that's who He is, that's His character -- love. And whatever you have gone through, and whatever healing is needed, God's love is available twenty-four hours a day, seven days a week to heal, restore, and renew.

My sweet friend, Teena Goble, describes God's love as liquid love—love that pours into every nook and cranny of our lives. The description is perfect. God's love is pure, infusing, total and complete. His love flows like streams in a desert. There is no area too barren or removed for the touch of God's love.

God's love endures forever. His love is faithful, just, righteous, merciful, abounding in love, great, everlasting to everlasting, gracious, compassionate, slow to anger, rich, covenant of love, love that makes deserts bloom, love that reaches to the heavens, living water love, the love of Christ is wide, long, high, and deep, love that floods the soul with healing, unfailing love.

And God loves you – just as you are ... wounded, battered, bruised. God loves you – your past, the hidden things no one knows. God loves you – your jagged scars that carved valleys in your soul.

God loves you – and no one and nothing can keep Him from you. No person. No power on earth. No memory. No flashback. No sin. No thought. No action. Nothing can stop God from offering His healing and His everlasting, unfailing love.

The One who made you, the One who loves you with an unfailing love, He is The One who wants to heal you and The One who can heal you.

Step 2 - Relay Honest Information

Go to God. Be honest with how you feel, how your wounds affect you, how they changed your life. If you're angry, don't understand, howling mad, or shell-shocked, be honest with God. Jesus says to worship The Father in Spirit and Truth. For when we honestly come to God with how deeply we have been wounded, how terrible the situation, the sin from ourselves or others, we have taken steps to exposure and on to healing.

If you are angry at God for what happened to you, your loved ones, your job, your family, your home, your childhood, your life, whatever has happened to cause your wounds ... talk to God. Be truthful and the Lord will be there and near.

Without The Truth, we can't come to the Father. Jesus said, "I am the way and the truth and the life. No one comes to the Father except through me." ~ John 14:6

Without The Truth, the Holy Spirit can't guide. "The Spirit of truth will guide you into all the truth. He will not speak on his own; he will speak only what he hears, and he will tell you what is yet to come." ~ John 16:13

Without The Truth, we can't live in freedom. Jesus said, "If you hold to my teaching, you are really my disciples. Then you will know the truth, and the truth will set you free." ~ John 8:31-32

Without Truth, we can't enter into God's presence. "Lord, who may dwell in your sacred tent? Who may live on your holy mountain? The one whose walk is blameless, who does what is righteous, who speaks the truth from their heart; whose tongue utters no slander, who does no wrong to a neighbor, and casts no slur on others." ~ Psalm 15:1-3

Without The Truth, we can't worship. "God is Spirit and His worshipers must worship in Spirit and truth." ~ John 4:24

Without The Truth, we live in darkness. In the Truth we live in the light and illuminating God. "Whoever lives by the truth comes into the light, so that it may be seen plainly that what they have done has been done in the sight of God." ~ John 3:21

In The Truth we delight God and are blessed with His wisdom. "You delight in truth in the inward being and You teach me wisdom in the secret heart." ~ Psalm 51:6

Be a soul-wrestler. Find the truth. When you want to understand why something bothers or makes your soul disquieted, go to God. When things don't make sense, makes you troubled, fearful, anxious, or depressed, whatever brings darkness, find the light in God's truth. For in God's truth we receive the blessings of understanding.

Jacob wrestled with God, and he wouldn't let go until he received a blessing. He leaves us with some good ideas on how to deal with problems.

"Jacob stayed behind by himself, and a man wrestled with him until daybreak. When the man saw that he couldn't get the best of Jacob as they wrestled, he deliberately threw Jacob's hip out of joint. The man said, 'Let me go; it's daybreak.' Jacob said, 'I'm not letting you go 'til you bless me.' The man said, 'What's your name?' He answered, 'Jacob.' The man said, 'But no longer. Your name is no longer Jacob. From now on its Israel (God-Wrestler); you've wrestled with God, and you've come through.' ... And then, right then and there, he blessed him. Jacob named the place Peniel (God's Face) because, he said, 'I saw God face-to-face and lived to tell the story!'" ~ Genesis 32:24-30 MSG

There are blessings in the wrestling, the not letting go. The wrestling to venture beyond the quick, addictive temporary "fixes" of this world, or the shrugging of shoulders and caving in to believe the enemy lies. The blessings come when we wrestle until the dawn of understanding breaks.

When the soul becomes disquieted, when the heartbeat runs amok with fears and worries, run to wrestle the darkness out of your soul. Search God's word; take your concerns to your Heavenly Father. Ask Him to break through. And He will. He does.

When you seek God with your heart, you'll find Him in your heart. And in His heart, the blessing of His light shines.

You don't have to clean up – yourself, your prayer, or your request. God already knows your thoughts and He wants you to honestly come to Him, because in that honesty, in the truth, you can approach His throne, and in the presence of Truth, lies are revealed, the blessings come, and healing flows free.

Step 3 - Allow Treatment

Some are afraid to heal because that's all they've ever known. The Bible tells us, in the fifth chapter of John, a man had been an invalid for thirty-eight years. This man and many others--the blind, lame, and paralyzed--laid by the pool of Bethesda. This was no ordinary pool; for there were times the water would be stirred by an angel, and the first one in would be healed. Day after day this man and others would watch and wait for a miracle.

And then in walks Jesus. He knew how long the man had been lying there, he knew how desperate his condition. And yet Jesus asks, "Do you want to be made well?'"

"Sir," The man answered, "I have no man to put me into the pool when the water is stirred up, but while I am coming, another steps down before me."[i]

Did you realize, the man never answered Jesus' question?

And still, Jesus tells him to rise, take up his bed, and walk. And immediately the man was made well, took up his bed, and walked.

When Jesus comes into lives, change happens.

We cannot always choose what happened or is happening in our lives; however we do have an option how we respond. When we refuse to release our pain, infirmities, painful memories, wrongs committed against us, we become like the invalid, complaining no one is there to carry us—even as the Great Physician stands with His hand outstretched asking, "Do you want to get well?"

I've yet to meet a person who doesn't have a painful memory from something they did, or from something someone else said or did to them. I'm so grateful for God's spiritual cleansing and healing. However it's far too easy to become uncomfortably comfortable in the (un)comfort zone.

Don't get mucked in the muck of the pit of the past. Christ offers freedom. With the ladder of God's love, forgiveness, mercy, and grace, we can climb out of the mess of the past. We can leave behind the muck.

Wholeness through Christ comes one piece at a time when we give up every piece of ourselves to Him. And when we release our pieces, His peace comes. Give God you, and within Him you will find the amazing love and freedom that is freely given.

Regardless of when your wound happened, Jesus can heal. Regardless of when you became a Christian, Jesus can heal. Freedom and healing comes when wounds are released to God—completely and totally.

Picture you've been in a horrific accident, your body is mangled, and your entire family has been affected by the fault of another person. The ambulance arrives to take you to the Hospital. The best doctor in the world and the finest medical staff are on alert waiting just for you.

You can choose not to go.

The other person was at fault, and you want the world to see what they did to you. You want everyone to see your deep wounds and scars.

You have the choice to refuse treatment and sit with your wounds, moan, and groan how unfair life is, wondering why the wounds stay so deep and so painful. Or you can go to the Great Physician who will take every injury, wrap them tenderly and lovingly with His healing touch.

God is a God of tender, compassionate, and unfailing love. He knows how deep the wounds. He knows how terrible the hurt. He leans down to heal the brokenhearted and bind up wounds. Freedom and healing come when we give our past to God—completely and totally. Remove the excuses, go to God for your healing, and allow His treatment. He is waiting.

But you don't know how bad it was or is. Give it to God – He upholds the cause of the oppressed and sets the prisoners free. ~ Psalm 146:7

I can't forgive. Give it to God - If you forgive men when they sin against you, your heavenly Father will also forgive you. But if you do not forgive men their sins, your Father will not forgive your sins. ~ Matthew 6:14-15

I need to tell them how much they hurt me, how wrong they were, I want my pound of flesh. Give it to God – Don't take revenge, but leave room for God's wrath, for it is written: 'It is mine to avenge; I will repay,' says the Lord. ~ Romans 12:19

I'm so weak. Give it to God - He gives strength to His people; He blesses His people with peace. ~ Psalm 29:11

I'm too afraid. Give it to God – Jesus gives you peace. Don't let your hearts be troubled and don't be afraid. ~ John 14:27

There is too much sorrow. Give it to God – He has tenderly captured every tear you have cried. ~ Psalm 56:6

But I can't do it without help. Give it to God – You can do everything through Him who gives strength" ~ Philippians 4:13

But I need to talk about it more, I need more sympathy, I need more time, nobody understands... Give it to God – Cast your cares on Him. He will sustain you. He won't let the righteous fall. He is good and a refuge in times of trouble. He cares for those who trust Him. ~ Psalm 55:22, Nahum 1:7

God is enough. Trust Him. He is greater than the past, and greater than any problem, circumstance, or person.

God understands. He cares. God has the ears, the arms, the legs, the strength, the might, the justice, the vengeance, the counsel, the comfort, the healing, the peace, the joy, and the life everlasting.

Release the past to God—He is enough for your healing. He beckons those who are weary and burdened to come to Him. In Him you will find rest.[ii]

Step 4 - Let The Light Shine

Expose wounds, that darkness, to God's healing light.

There are dark closets in many souls, the ones containing broken places, or the areas someone hurt, used, or took away innocence. The place where sins are hidden. Or perhaps those containing personal and bystander carnage from traveling wrong roads.

I had a room full of closets. The doors weren't only bolted but walled up behind concrete barriers. I thought ignoring reality worked in an odd way. Unfortunately suppressing memories only allowed them to fester or ooze out in strange and unsightly mutations. They never healed.

With God's tender nudging, the time finally came for major cleaning. God gently prodded me forward to deal with areas I had only allowed Band-Aid applications.

I didn't go quietly. I went kicking and screaming. I wrestled and fought with God, afraid if I ventured into the past, even with Him, perhaps I would drown in horrifying memories and never be able to return.

I felt like I was being pushed off a thousand foot bridge over a black river filled with hungry crocodiles. Yes, I knew God was with me, but I didn't know how far into the deep I'd have to go. What if my tether broke? And what if I couldn't come back?

Then I dreamt Jesus was holding my hand and walking me through my past, allowing me to see how He was there, and how He loved and cared for me through the moments of abuse, and then how His presence heals all wounds. The process was painful, but only because of my own unfounded fears.

God has walked me through an abundance of issues and hurts, and each time the fear lessens, and the anticipation grows. Now when I sense His beckoning to go deeper, I might whimper a touch, yet rejoice as God steps me forward in the process to become whole and more like His precious Son, Jesus.

As God tenderly pulls away layers concealed in darkness, His light cleanses, renews, and brings wonderful freedom. Because there is no memory too dark, no sin too hidden, and no abuse too great, for the healing touch of God.

When my friend Angela underwent shoulder surgery and couldn't hold her brand-new grandbaby, friends came to help. One friend put her arms around Angela so that they could put the baby in her friend's arms, then they nestled that baby against Angela's chest. In the same way, God puts His arms around our wounded hearts and nourishes and nurtures us back to wholeness.

When God asks us to return with Him to clean out our past, He's not asking us to bungee jump into the darkness. He is allowing the release of our wounds to His healing hands, the shining of His light on the darkness, the exposure of the lies to God's truth. He's asking us to trust enough to leap into His arms, where we are healed, and fly forever free.

Submit to God's healing; allow the gunk, bad tissue, drainage, and waste products to be removed. Allow His Sword of the Spirit to scalpel through until healthy tissue is found.

Don't allow the lies of the enemy to keep you in bondage. Please don't allow a view of God's Truth to be obscured by society, family, or friends. Don't allow the desire to be accepted by friends, family, and society to stand in the way of living for Christ. Through following, loving, and obeying Christ, knowing His truth, knowing His word, The Truth can be clearly seen. For in God's Truth is the freedom of The Truth of God's Truth and in His light we find healing.

Please read the following lies and truth and make note of any truths you need to remember.

The enemy lies, "You shouldn't have been born. You are a mistake."

God's Truth ~ This is what the LORD says, who saved you, who formed you in your mother's body: I, the LORD, made everything, stretching out the skies by myself and spreading out the earth all alone. Before I made you in your mother's womb, I chose you. Before you were born, I set you apart for a special work. I say this because I know what I am planning for you. I have good plans for you, not plans to hurt you. I will give you hope and a good future. ~ Isaiah 44:24, Jeremiah 1:5, 29:11.

The enemy lies, "No one loves or wants you."

God's Truth ~ I have loved you with an everlasting love; I have drawn you to myself with loving-kindness. I love you. For as high as the heavens are above the earth, so great is My steadfast love toward those who fear Me. Long before I laid down earth's foundations, I had you in mind, had settled as the focus of My love, to be made whole and holy by My love. Long, long ago I decided to adopt you into My family through Jesus Christ. (What pleasure I took in planning this!) I wanted you to enter into the celebration of My lavish gift-giving by the hand of My beloved Son. It's in Christ that you find out who you are and what you are living for. Long before you first heard of Christ and got your hopes up, I had My eye on you, had designs on you for glorious living, part of the overall purpose I am working out in everything and everyone. ~ Jeremiah 31:3, John 15:9, Psalm 103:11, Ephesians 1:3-6, 11-12 MSG.

The enemy lies, "You are alone."

God's Truth ~ Do not be afraid or discouraged, for I will personally go ahead of you. I will be with you; I will neither fail you nor abandon you. Don't be afraid, for I am with you. Don't be discouraged, for I am your God. I will strengthen you and help you. I will hold you up with my victorious right hand. When you pass through the waters, I will be with you; and through the rivers, they shall not overwhelm you; when you walk through fire you shall not be burned, and the flame shall not consume you. For the I AM living among you. I am a mighty savior. I take delight in you with gladness. With My love, I will calm all your fears. I will rejoice over you with joyful songs. ~ Deuteronomy 31:8 NLT Isaiah 41:10 NLT, Isaiah 43:2 ESV, Zephaniah 3:17 NLT.

The enemy lies, "You've gone too far from God's grace."

God's Truth ~ My power is enough to save you. I hear when you ask Me for help. My mercy is great, and I love you very much. Though you were spiritually dead because of the things you did against Me, I give you new life with Christ. You have been saved by My grace. And I've raised you up with Christ and gave you a seat with Him in the heavens. I did this for those in Christ Jesus so that for all future time I can show the very great riches of My grace by being kind to you in Christ Jesus. You have been saved by grace through believing. You did not save yourselves; it was a gift from Me. I rescued you from dead-end alleys and dark dungeons. I've set you up in the kingdom of the Son I love so much the Son who got you out of the pit you were in, got rid of the sins you were doomed to keep repeating. ~ Isaiah 59:1 NCV, Ephesians 2:4-8 NCV, Colossians 1:13-14 MSG.

The enemy lies, "Your wounds are too deep."

God's Truth ~ I came to heal the broken-hearted and heal their wounds, set the captives free and release the oppressed, the things that are impossible with people are possible with Me. I made the heavens and the earth by My great power and outstretched arm, nothing is too hard for Me. For you who fear My name, the sun of righteousness will rise with healing in its wings; and you will go forth and skip about like calves from the stall. ~ Luke 4:18, Matthew 19:26, Jeremiah 32:17, Malachi 4:2

The enemy lies, "No one understands you."

God's truth ~ I know when you sit down and when you get up. I know your thoughts before you think them. I have compassion on you. I know how you are formed and remember you are but dust. I know and understand you. ~ Psalm 139:2 Psalm 103:13-14, Jeremiah 9:24.

The enemy lies, "There is no hope or help."

God's truth ~ I am your Creator. I am the one who formed you. Don't fear, I have redeemed you. I have called you by name; you are Mine! When you pass through the waters, I will be with you; and through the rivers, they will not overflow you. When you walk through the fire, you will not be scorched, nor will the flame burn you. For I am the LORD your God, the Holy One of Israel, your Savior. Your help comes from the Me, the Maker of heaven and earth. I will not let your foot slip. I watch over you and do not slumber. I'm your shade at your right hand. The sun won't harm you by day, nor the moon by night. I will keep you from all harm. I will watch over your life. I'll watch over your coming and going now and forever. I am your help and your shield. Your soul finds rest in Me. Your hope comes from Me. ~ Psalm 33:20, 62:5, 121, Isaiah 43:1-3

The enemy lies, "You are unprotected."

God's truth ~ My name is a strong tower, the righteous run to it and are safe. I am your hiding place. I will protect you from trouble and surround you with songs of deliverance. I am faithful, and I will strengthen and protect you from the evil one. I will cover you with My feathers, and under My wings you will find refuge; My faithfulness will be your shield and rampart. I am your rock, fortress and deliverer. I am your rock, in whom you take refuge. I am your shield and stronghold. ~ Proverbs 18:10, Psalm 32:7, 2 Thessalonians 3:3, Psalm 91:4, Psalm 18:2.

The enemy lies, "Nothing good will come from this."

God's Truth ~ I will comfort you, so you will be able to comfort others with the comfort with which I give you. Your comfort is abundant through Christ. Consider it all joy when you encounter various trials, because the testing of your faith produces endurance. And let endurance have its perfect result, so you may be perfect and complete, lacking in nothing. Though now for a little while you may have had to suffer grief in all kinds of trials. These have come so that your faith—of greater worth than gold, which perishes even though refined by fire—may be proved genuine and may result in praise, glory and honor when Jesus Christ is revealed. You are blessed when you persevere under trial; for once you have been approved, you will receive the crown of life which I have promised to those who love Me. For I will cause all things to work together for good to those who love Me, to those who are called according to My purpose. ~ 2 Corinthians 1:3-5 NASB, James 1:2-4 NASB, 1 Peter 1:6-7 NIV, James 1:12 NASB

You were formed and created by the God of the universe. In Christ, you are forgiven and free from condemnation and shame, redeemed, restored, renewed, complete, and loved forever. And, that's the God-given truth!

"You will know the truth, and the truth will set you free. Being confident of this, that He who began a good work in you will carry it on to completion until the day of Christ Jesus." (John 8:32, Philippians 1:6 NIV)

Step 5 - Inside Out Healing

Wounds must heal from the inside out. Inside Jesus we find that healing.

A friend shared lies her mom had spoken over her from childhood. Mean, nasty, life-altering lies that had kept my friend in bondage most of her life. And as she was sharing, another friend, said, "The pain is too much."

Your pain may be too much for a human to carry. That's why we have Jesus. That's why He came, and that's why He's here for you. That's why He wants to heal your hurt.

Because He is the one who made your heart and with His love He can restore and remake anything and anyone.

Regardless of how deep the past, regardless of how painful what happened, or what even may be happening now. Regardless of the lies, regardless of the half-truths spoken over you, Jesus is The Truth – the whole truth.

The pain is too much - that's why Jesus went to the cross.

The pain is too much - that's why He carries your burden.

The pain is too much - that's why He heals the broken-hearted and binds their wounds.

The pain is too much - that's why He captures every precious tear you cry, and He will wipe every tear from your eyes.

The pain is too much - that's why He gives you power to overcome by His blood and the word of your testimony.

The pain is too much - that's why He loves you enough to carry you, that's why He will take everything you have gone through, every painful moment, and will turn it to good. And that's why He won't ever leave you or forsake you.

The pain is too much - that's why He came to earth, that's why He died for you, that's why He conquered death and rose again, that's why He offers eternal hope, and that's why He is here, right now, holding you close.

The pain is too much - that's why He is the healer, restorer, and redeemer. That's why we have Jesus.

The pain of sin (ours and others) is too much, yet because of the sacrifice, mercy, and grace of Jesus we are given new life. His grace. His forgiveness is the key to eternal life and the key to our healing.

Wounds must heal from the inside out, and inside Jesus you find your healing.

Step 6 - Forgiveness

Jesus said, "If you forgive men when they sin against you, your heavenly Father will also forgive you. But if you do not forgive men their sins, your Father will not forgive your sins."[iii]

Forgiveness is a **huge** key to our healing. And forgiveness involves several layers – forgiveness of others and forgiveness of ourselves.

Forgiving Others

When God tells us to forgive others, He is not questioning the reality of your wounds, or the level of your pain, or that you have been sinned against. Forgiveness is not what you do for them; it is a gift to yourself. And with that gift comes, freedom, peace of mind, and right fellowship and relationship with God. Forgiveness does not release their debt. Forgiveness of others releases our debt.

God tells us to forgive; we must do so--regardless of the sin. He has forgiven us, we must forgive others. The world responds that there is justification in not forgiving, or that God is callous by requiring forgiveness, but please remember your forgiveness of others does not excuse their sin. Your forgiveness does not make their sin null and void—they still have to stand before God. God does not forget their sin when you forgive them.

Holocaust survivor, Corrie Ten Boom wrote, "Since the end of the war I had a home in Holland for victims of Nazi brutality. Those who were able to forgive their former enemies were able also to return to the outside world and rebuild their lives, no matter what the physical scars. Those who nursed bitterness remained invalids. It was as simple and as horrible as that."

When Jesus died on the cross, He said to the Father, "Unto You I commit My spirit."[iv] Forgiveness is an act of yielding. It is saying to God "Unto You I commit the wrong committed against me." It is giving over, yielding to God, so you can live free. So you can rise from the ashes of your past.

Picture a courtroom. The jury is in place, the lawyers are ready, and the judge sits on the bench. The person who wronged you is brought in. You jump to your feet, and you hit that person over and over again. They deserve punishment. They didn't give you mercy, and you show no mercy. The bailiff and lawyers try to restrain you, but to no avail.

You scream and point at the offender, "That person does not deserve forgiveness."

The judge bangs his gavel and pronounces his verdict, "As you have spoken, so it will be done. If that person doesn't deserve forgiveness, neither do you."

Our choices are limited. We can forgive others and be forgiven. Or we can keep a tally of their sins. The problem is, our sins continue to be tallied.

Which sin do you want remaining on your record?

The person most hurt by not forgiving - you.

If you don't forgive, you remain chained to your offender, continually offended by that offense, and that experience.

When you refuse to forgive, when you continue to wallow in the wrongs committed to you, you are refusing the blood of the lamb—the blood that is deep enough, red enough, cleansing enough, to heal and erase the hurt, the anger, and the frustrations. You have to release it to God. Not part, not just a little, but all. You can be chained to your heartache and your unforgiving spirit, or you can be released today.

God will punish the guilty. No sin goes unnoticed. Repeat that. No. Sin. Goes. Unnoticed. God knows everything they did and thought. He knows what we did and did not do. God keeps watch on the wicked and the good.[v] Jesus promises, there is nothing covered that will not be revealed, and hidden that will not be known.[vi] And He will punish the guilty.

Unfortunately I know a person who is still angry at someone who has been dead for decades. Anger has done nothing but stagnate growth—causing bitterness, illness, and a lack of connection with those around them. I have seen people turn into a version of the very person they hated, because that is what consumed them -- that is who they thought about, and that is what they became.

An unforgiving spirit fouls up everything—including attitudes, and relationships with others and with God. The garbage of unforgiveness is heavy, depressing, smelly, stinky, and rots from the inside out.

Through Christ, we find the power to forgive, and through Him we receive our healing. Release your burden to Him. Not part, not just a little, but all. You can be chained to your heartache and your unforgiving spirit, or you can be released today.

Let's replay the courtroom scenario. The date arrives and the person who wronged you appears before the judge. You forgive—not because the person deserves forgiveness—you forgive because Christ has forgiven you.

The judge listens quietly and pronounces his verdict. The person who wronged you is convicted. With a righteous Judge, the punishment always fits the crime. Forgiveness unlocks the chains that chained you. Jesus reaches out with compassion, mercy, and grace. Forgive, and you will be forgiven.[vii]

Justice is served, and you walk free.

Forgiving Ourselves

Sometimes forgiving others is easier than forgiving ourselves. My sins and failures are many. I'm horrified and embarrassed at some of the choices I made in the past.

Temptation presented itself as an ocean of delight. I stood on the edge thinking perhaps I could dip just a toe in and no one would notice, and surely no one would get hurt. However at the slightest step, I found myself in over my head in a slime pit of slime, covered in the mud of sin. And nothing could remove those stains. Nothing and no one, except the mercy and grace of Jesus.

Don't let the enemy convince you that your sin is too bad, too many, or too terrible for God's forgiveness. Or you have to get your life in order and get yourself clean before you can be saved or useful in God's kingdom.

The enemy (or our own conscience) replays failures over and over again or others won't allow us to move on and forget. But remember you don't need to fear or run and hide because God knows about every sin, every thought, and every action that you have done. He knows about your yesterday, today, and tomorrow. And still He offers grace and mercy.

I've heard people say that because of their sins there is no hope for repair or restoration. Yes, there are always consequences to sin. And unfortunately behaviors will spill over to affect other lives.

Fortunately, God is bigger than any mistake or failure.

David was an adulterer and murderer. But God called him a man after His own heart.

Moses killed a man. But God spoke to him face-to-face.

Rahab was a prostitute. But God blessed her to be the mother of Boaz. And Boaz married Ruth, and through their further generations came our precious Savior, Jesus Christ.

Saul stood by watching and agreeing with the stoning of Steven and then he persecuted Christians. But God used him in mighty ways to further His kingdom.

The woman caught in adultery, the woman who "lived a sinful life" all found forgiveness at the feet of Jesus.

Regardless of your past, no matter what has happened, what you have been through, God's forgiveness is freely offered for those who come to Him.

Let that steep in you. The Lord will forgive if you honestly, earnestly confess, and repent.

Grace touches to the very marrow of our being and cleanses us from the inside out, creating a new creature in Christ. Created uniquely, we become the best we can be through His grace. All we must do is accept what He so freely offers.

Jesus said, "It is finished."[viii] The definition of finished is "Paid in full." When Jesus went to the cross He paid the price for your sins. He paid the debt for you. Every one of your sins paid on the cross by the sacrifice of Jesus. His grace covers you.

Forgiveness is a Holy God reaching out through the outstretched hands of His precious son Jesus, where all your sins were nailed to the cross. A lifetime could be lost in striving for unachievable perfection, but God's forgiveness is instantaneous.

Let God's forgiveness wash over you. He forgives your sins and throws them as far as the east is to the west. He remembers them no more. God beckons, "I have swept away your sins like a cloud. I have scattered your offenses like the morning mist. Oh, return to me, for I have paid the price to set you free." ~ Isaiah 44:22 NLT

Accept God's forgiveness for yourself and for others. His grace and mercy covers you.

If you would be willing, take a rock and hold it in the palms of your outstretched hands. This rock will symbolize the burden you have held on to, the spirit of unforgiveness for yourself or others. Close your eyes and picture Christ hanging on the cross for the sins of the world and for your sins.

Now picture Christ as the risen Lord who conquered sin and death standing with his arms open waiting for you to come to Him in freedom. Give your burden to God by symbolically dropping the rock in the hands of Jesus.

Release your burden. Let go of the anger, hurt, and bitterness, and give it to God.

Ask God right now to release the chains that have held you captive. Give God the memory, the pain, forgive the offender, forgive yourself, ask God to forgive you. Place the burden once and for all in His hands, and then ask Him to fill the space that memory occupied with His Holy Spirit and the light and love of the Lord Jesus Christ.

The moment you do, drop the rock, let it fall, hear the sound of your freedom as you fly unburdened straight to God's love.

Step 7 - No Picking

Stop picking and stop allowing the enemy to pick. Don't pick at your wounds. Don't be a picker! Don't keep examining, and wondering, and mourning, and worrying. Don't let the enemy keep taunting. Don't play "that" song, "that" movie, TV show, or video. If it is in your power, don't keep company with people who drag you down or remind you of old wounds. If it is in your power, tell those you do live with, or hang around, not to remind you of old wounds.

Remember the old cartoons with the Coyote and the Road Runner? The Coyote would order every gadget imaginable from ACME to help him catch the Road Runner. Unfortunately either the products would fail, or the coyote's own incompetence would result in rather unappealing calamities.

Often the coyote would use an anvil in hopes of squashing the road runner. Instead, the anvil usually fell right back on the coyote's head.

Lugging around past issues without allowing for God's healing never has positive results. You might as well strap an anvil to your back.

Don't lose another moment. Stop living in the "what if...", "what did," and "what might have been." Live today -- right now -- this moment. Allow yourself to be set free by The One who is freedom.

Have you seen dogs that have to wear the cones to keep them from picking at their sores? Let's put on the cone of God's truth.

Neil Anderson wrote, "Since Satan's primary weapon is the lie, your defense against him is the truth. Dealing with Satan is not a power encounter; it's a truth encounter. When you expose Satan's lie with God's truth, his power is broken."

Every time a memory returns, every time a nightmare happens, go to God's truth and praise Him, because God's truth and praise sends the enemy running. Praise God that no memory is too big for God. Praise God that no wound is too deep for God.

And in God's truth we find our freedom.

When we moved to Idaho, we visited the Old Idaho State Prison. It had opened its doors in 1870 and continued to operate until 1973. During the years of operation 13,000 convicts went in and out of those doors. And one of those convicts was Harry Orchard.

Orchard began his sentence in 1908 after being convicted of the assassination of a former governor of Idaho. Years later, due to good behavior, Orchard was paroled. But Orchard chose to stay and eventually died in 1954. Our tour guide surmised that perhaps Harry had enemies on the outside or no longer knew how to live beyond the prison walls.

Harry Orchard had a choice for freedom, and we too have a choice.

When we chose Christ, we choose freedom. Through Christ we are washed clean. Innocence is regained, and what was once lost is restored.

Please visualize the process. The God who created the universe offers total and complete restoration. You chose Christ. Every bad thought, every evil action, and every evil touch, taken away. Every bit of sin is forgiven and removed. Every spot made pure. You are wholly recreated in Christ. When God looks at you, He sees His perfect Son.

Your prison cell is open, and you are free.

However many people are locked in the past unable to move forward. The enemy might try to convince you that you aren't free, but remember Jesus stands at the door to your freedom.

And now, once you are a Christian, He stands at the door to block you from going back to the past.

Those bad memories? You don't have to go back; Jesus stands at the door.

Those failures? They're gone, Jesus stands at the door.

Those sins? They're cleansed, Jesus stands at the door.

Don't listen to Satan's lies you can never be free, or your innocence never regained. Don't believe the enemy who was behind all the evil in the first place!

The cell door is open, and Jesus stands at the door.

Jesus picks you for freedom. The only picking you need to do is to pick up the mercy and grace of Jesus.

Step 8 - Wound Cauterization

In the Old Testament, the Israelites had to offer sacrifices for their sins. And that sacrifice gave them the visual of the flames consuming the sin that stood in the way of a relationship with a righteous and holy God.

The smell, the smoke rising to Heaven, and the knowledge of that release, although probably painful to watch had to be very freeing.

If there are things you have had trouble releasing -- things you have done or things others have done to you – if you would be willing, write those things down. Not to relive the pain, but to write them to God.

Take it to God, write it out, write all that has happened, everything that is bothering you, everything you can't forgive, and everything that continues to torment, and take them to God.

Read it aloud, cry, wail, and tell Him exactly how you feel about what happened, how you feel about everything. And as you read it out loud, as you talk to Him, ask Him to help you forgive, and lay it on His altar.

And then, if you have a safe place, burn those pages. Burn them. Watch the fire consume everything written, smell and watch the smoke as it rises to Heaven. As the edges of the papers curl, the words disintegrate; you will have a visual of your freedom.

Now when the enemy taunts you with past mistakes or tries to have you walk back down the pathway to your past wounds, you'll be able to remember those items have been given to God where everything falls under His justice, righteousness, and grace.

Step 9 - Scar Beauty

Realize the beauty of your scars. Your broken pieces allow God to shine through. The rubble becomes a platform, the mess becomes a message, and the test becomes a testimony.

My friend, Patricia is a fused-glass artist. Sitting on my dresser is a six inch cross she made from seventy-five tiny pieces of glass. Some glass changes when it's fired in the furnace, so each piece was individually chosen, hand-cut, and perfectly shaped. No mold is used, and no two are exactly alike. She stands all those small glass pieces up and then places them in the kiln and it fires. The process and product is amazing, the ordinary glass becomes a work of art.

I didn't want any of my bad pieces. I wanted to hide them away, throw them out, or pretend they didn't exist. But remember those glass pieces which are one color before the furnace? The fire brings out new hues, depth, and beauty. God is the artist. He takes our messed up lives, mends our wounds, and with His unfailing love fires through the broken pieces and creates beauty.

George Mueller wrote, "In a thousand trials, it is not just five hundred of them that work 'for the good' of the believer, but nine hundred and ninety-nine, plus one."

No moment of your time, pain, or suffering is ever wasted.

And you, as a work of art, will help others be drawn to the magnificent work God does with broken pieces.

Step 10 – Prevention

Prevent enemy attacks; prevent the nightmares and memories by filling up with God's word. What has been emptied, must be filled. What has been cleaned and released, needs to stay cleansed. Keep your mind and thoughts clean by knowing God's truth. Stay in His word.

Paul advises us to fix our thoughts on what is true, honorable, right, pure, lovely, admirable, and to think about things that are excellent and worthy of praise. And to be anxious for nothing, but in everything by prayer and supplication with thanksgiving let our requests be made known to God. And there we will find the peace of God, which surpasses all comprehension, to guard our hearts and minds in Christ Jesus.

When negative thoughts come calling, take them captive! When a thought comes in, run it through the filter of God's truth. If that thought wouldn't please God, kick it out. If those words wouldn't please God, don't say them.

Just because that thought sounds like your voice, it isn't, the enemy is always trying to plant ideas, depressing feedback, and keep the focus on wounds, problems, and anything negative.

Refocus your focus on the power, might, strength, loving-kindness, and compassion of God. The God who defeats all foes and turns mourning into joy, the God who takes everything the enemy meant for evil and turns it into good.

God's word tells us to enter His courts with praise and thanksgiving ~ Psalm 100:4.

Praise and thanksgiving brings us into God's presence. Praise and thanksgiving breaks through barriers – barriers erected by the enemy, by ourselves, by others, by our circumstances and situations. Praise and thanksgiving refocuses the focus, giving new eyes, granting fresh soul-air. Praise and thanksgiving provides restoration and renewal.

P – Praise
A – And
T – Thanksgiving

Praise and thanksgiving points us back to our inexhaustible power-source, all-powerful God. So today, this very minute, **PAT** away those negative thoughts. When the enemy beckons you to focus on your wounds, respond with praise and thanksgiving for who our God is, for what He has done, and for His eternal love, grace, and mercy.[ix]

Another way to keep your defenses strong against enemy attacks it to read and know God's word. Going beyond surface knowledge, to knowing God and His character. Knowing who He is, His all-encompassing authority, His amazing strength, power, mercy, and love, giving the allegiance to stand firm, and diving to the depths of the true knowledge of God.

Hosea 4:6 reminds us that God's people are often destroyed from lack of knowledge. But Daniel 11:32 tells us that the people who know their God will prove themselves strong, stand firm, and accomplish mighty exploits.

There is power in God's Word, power to find His grace and mercy, power to heal, and power to be strong.

Be like Paul and say, "I know (perceive, have knowledge of, and am acquainted with) Him Whom I have believed (adhered to and trusted in and relied on), and I am [positively] persuaded that He is able to guard and keep that which has been entrusted to me and which I have committed [to Him]." ~ 2 Timothy 1:12 AMP

Taking thoughts captive isn't just about shoving them behind bars; it is exploring God's truth and finding the reality of God's might, power, forgiveness, mercy, and grace. Total freedom comes from, and in, God's truth. Knowing (truly knowing) God's word demolishes the lies and bad thoughts.

The sword of the Spirit cuts off the enemy's lies. "...Jesus said, if you hold to my teaching, you are really my disciples. Then you will know the truth, and the truth will set you free. For I will give you utterance and wisdom which none of your opponents will be able to resist or refute." ~ John 8:31-32 NIV, Luke 21:15 NLT

Pray, study, and learn, ask God to, "Send forth your light and your truth, let them guide me." ~ Psalm 43:3 NIV

Take every thought captive, wrap it in God's truth, throw it out, smash it, destroy it, and live free. For, "You are from God, little children, and have overcome them; because greater is He who is in you than he who is in the world." ~ 1 John 4:4 NASB

Remember, use powerful God-tools for smashing warped philosophies, tearing down barriers erected against the truth of God, fitting every loose thought and emotion and impulse into the structure of life shaped by Christ." ~ 2 Corinthians 10:5 MSG

Know God by spending time with God, pray, listen, and cuddle into His heart. Know God and seek His face. The more You know God, the greater the freedom, the firmer the foundation, the more fruit bearing, and the more radical, joy-filled, exploit living life!

"Because of this, since the day we heard about you, we have continued praying for you, asking God that you will know fully what he wants. We pray that you will also have great wisdom and understanding in spiritual things so that you will live the kind of life that honors and pleases the Lord in every way. You will produce fruit in every good work and grow in the knowledge of God." ~ Colossians 1:9-10 NCV.

Step 11 - The Divine Rescue

Realize the benefits of submitting to healing because your wounds, your soul-scars, are part of an amazing reality – the divine rescue.

Remember the story of Joseph? He was sold into slavery by his brothers, falsely accused of rape, imprisoned for years, and then elevated to second in command under Pharaoh. Later Joseph told his brothers what they meant for evil, God used for the saving of many lives.

Joseph's life, what happened to him, and his ultimate rescue, continues to save lives. His story gives hope that even when bad things happen, good will come. The Bible contains true-life situations and true-life rescues. And now, I tape weekly messages of true-life lives that have been through fires or discovered God's truth in wonderful ways; telling others that God's rescue continues. And through their stories they continue to rescue lives.

And your story will be part of a divine rescue that ripples wider than you can imagine.

God never wastes our time or our pain. Never.

God's plans are so much bigger than we can imagine or even see.

God's glory is displayed in the back-against-the-Red-Sea moments, in the lion's den, the fiery furnaces, and in the battle scars of life. Afflictions, adversities, trials, troubles, and suffering, drive us to our knees and straight to God's heart. For in His loving heart we find all we need.

Through the fires of life, through the pain, the highs the lows, the loss and the gain, God refines us and draws us closer to His heart. And as He works with us and through us, more will come to know Him.

And oh what joy to know that nothing was wasted and that lives will be touched, and souls saved.

And in the end, every drop of heartache will be replaced with unending joy!

God delivers your soul from death, your eyes from tears, your feet from stumbling. He will go before you and be with you. He will never leave or forsake you. Don't be afraid or discouraged. And in the end, He will wipe every tear from your eyes, and there will be no more death, sorrow, crying, or pain. All those things will be gone forever.[x]

Step 12 - Be A Physician's Assistant

Now be a Physician's Assistant, take what the enemy meant for evil and smash it right back on his slimy head.

Revelation 12:11 shares, "...They overcame him (the enemy) because of the blood of the Lamb and because of the word of their testimony."

When the enemy throws stink bombs, God blows back the stink to restore, renew, and use everything for good. And when we allow God to walk us through and provide soul healing, He uses our difficulties to help in the battle for others.

What better way to defeat the enemy than by turning the evil used against us to provide freedom for others? All around us, people are dying – mentally, physically, and spiritually. And our stories may well be part of their rescue.

What the enemy used to hurt you, throw back on him, heap the mess right back on his slimy head by allowing God to heal you and then share your testimony. Don't hide what God has done in your life. Don't let the pain the enemy caused you to be wasted. Use it for God's glory. And use it to torment the tormentor.

Use the rubble of your past as a platform to set other captives free. You can take those in need to God's care through intercessory prayer, you can be God's hands and feet to the wounded inside and out of the church.

Ann Voskamp's[xi] tender words beckon, "We need you — It is the wounded ones who makes us heal and the hurting ones who make us honest and it is the broken ones who put us back together again and it is the scarred ones who make the Body of Christ sensitive."

Oswald Chambers reminds us to, "Let the past sleep, but let it sleep on the bosom of Christ, and go out into the irresistible future with him."

God's love, God's healing, and God's restoring power is never limited. There is nothing impossible for God. His love is unfailing, and His grace is redeeming. There is no wound too deep for the deep love of Christ.

Reflection

With God all things are possible (Matthew 19:26). With Jesus in our lives, He not only gives us the ability for eternal life, but the ability to overcome. Read Revelation 12:11, how did they overcome the enemy?

Read Isaiah 43:18-19 and Philippians 3:13-14. God is constantly doing new things, recreating, and making whole, as we forget the former things, allow His healing, and press forward. What does God's word tell us we will receive?

Read Psalm 91. As you read through the verses, make them personal. What verses touch you the deepest?

Contemplate the following Scripture passage: "The Lord is close to the brokenhearted." (Psalm 34:18) Remember always God is close to you.

Consider the following two quotes...

"When you deal intimately with human beings ... you wonder at times if forgiveness is not as rare as hen's teeth. People bury hatchets but carefully tuck away the map which tells where their hidden weapon lies. We put our resentments in cold storage and then pull the switch to let them thaw out again. Our grudges are taken out to the lake to drown them—even the lake of prayer—and we end up giving them a swimming lesson. How often have we torn up the canceled note but hung on to the wastebasket that holds the pieces." ~ Lofton Hudson

"Since the end of the war I had had a home in Holland for victims of Nazi brutality. Those who were able to forgive their former enemies were able also to return to the outside world and rebuild their lives, no matter what the physical scars. Those who nursed bitterness remained invalids. It was as simple and as horrible as that." ~ Holocaust survivor, Corrie Ten Boom

Who do you need to forgive?

Regardless of your current situation or the difficulties in your past, if you look at your life as a divine rescue plan, what hope and possibilities does that give you through that perspective?

How can you see God working through your trials and suffering?

Based on Psalm 40:1-3, how can you see God's rescue of you helping others?

"I waited patiently for the LORD; He turned to me and heard my cry. He lifted me out of the slimy pit, out of the mud and mire; He set my feet on a rock and gave me a firm place to stand. He put a new song in my mouth, a hymn of praise to our God. Many will see and fear and put their trust in the LORD."

How important are the stories of others who have been through difficulties and held firm to their faith? Will you share yours?

When you need reminders of God's Love

God's tender words to you....

I have loved you with an everlasting love; I have drawn you with loving-kindness. I created your inmost being; I knit you together in your mother's womb.

I am with you, I am mighty to save. I take great delight in you, I will quiet you with My love, I will rejoice over you with singing. See, I have engraved you on the palms of My hands. I take delight in you. I am gracious and righteous; I am full of compassion. My eyes search the whole earth in order to strengthen those whose hearts are fully committed to Me.

In My unfailing love I will lead you. In My strength I will guide you to My holy dwelling. I will make known to you the path of life. In My presence is fullness of joy; in My right hand there are pleasures forever. Though the mountains be shaken, and the hills be removed, yet My unfailing love for you will not be shaken nor My covenant of peace be removed, because I have compassion on you.

For I know the plans I have for you, plans to prosper you and not to harm you, plans to give you hope and a future. When you call upon Me and come and pray to Me, I will listen to you.

You will seek Me and find Me when you seek Me with all your heart. I will be found by you. Before you call I will answer; while you are still speaking I will hear.

My unfailing love is priceless. Both high and low among men find refuge in the shadow of My wings. I am love. And My love is patient, love is kind, does not envy, does not boast, it is not proud. It is not rude, it is not self-seeking, it is not easily angered, it keeps no record of wrongs. Love does not delight in evil but rejoices with the truth. It always protects, always trusts, always hopes, always perseveres. My love never fails.

I loved the world (and you) so much that I gave My one and only Son, that when you believe in Him you won't perish but have eternal life. I called you into fellowship with My Son Jesus Christ, and I am faithful. Jesus came that you may have life and have it abundantly.

Here I am! I stand at the door and knock. If you hear My voice and open the door, I will come in and eat with you, and you with Me.

(Jeremiah 31:3, Psalm 139:13, Zephaniah 3:17, Isaiah 49:16, Psalm 149:4, Psalm 116:5, II Chronicles 16:9, Exodus 15:13, Psalm 16:11, Isaiah 54:10, Jeremiah 29:11-14a, Isaiah 65:24, Psalm 36:7, 1 Corinthians 13:4-8, John 3:16, 1 Corinthians 1:9, John 10:10, Revelation 3:20)

My heart has heard You say, 'Come and talk with Me.' And my heart responds, 'LORD, I am coming.
(Psalm 27:8, NLT)

No wound is too deep for the deep love of Christ.

Lisa Buffaloe is not a professional counselor. Please don't hesitate to contact doctors or counselors when needed. Reaching out for help is a blessing given by God.

These steps are merely ones Lisa found helpful in her journey to healing from past hurts.

About the Author

Lisa Buffaloe is an author, speaker, happily married wife, and mom. Lisa's past experiences—molestation by a baby-sitter, assault, rape by a doctor, divorce, being stalked, cancer, death of loved ones, multiple surgeries, and eleven years of chronic illness from Lyme Disease—bless her with a backdrop to share God's amazing love. God's love is unending and through Jesus Christ we find healing, restoration, and renewal.

Visit Lisa at ...
LisaBuffaloe.com
Twitter.com/lisabuffaloe
Facebook.com/lisabuffaloe

Books By Lisa Buffaloe
(Updated July 2023)

Fiction
The Masterpiece Beneath
Nadia's Hope (Hope and Grace Series, Book 1)
  Prodigal Nights (Hope and Grace Series, Book 2)
  Writing Her Heart (Hope and Grace Series, Book 3)
  The Discovery Chapter (Hope and Grace Series, Book 4)
  Open Lens (Hope and Grace Series, Book 5)
The Fortune
Grace for the Char-Baked

Non-Fiction
Float by Faith

Heart and Soul Medication
Time with The Timeless One
The Forgotten Resting Place
Present in His Presence
We Were Meant for Paradise
One Lit Step: Devotions for your journey
The Unnamed Devotional
Flying on His Wings
Unfailing Treasures
No Wound Too Deep for The Deep Love of Christ
Living Joyfully Free Devotional, (Volume 1)
Living Joyfully Free Devotional (Volume 2)

Thank you for reading

No Wound Too Deep
For the Deep Love Of Christ

Lisa Buffaloe

---

[i] John 5:7

[ii] Matthew 11:28-30

[iii] Matthew 6:14-15

[iv] Luke 23:46

[v] Proverbs 15:3

[vi] Matthew 10:26

[vii] Luke 6:37

[viii] John 19:30

[ix] John 10:10, John 16:33, Matthew 6:34, Philippians 4:8, Philippians 4:6-7, 2 Corinthians 10:5, Psalm 19:14, Ephesians 6:10, Psalm 145, Revelation 21:4

[x] Psalm 116:8, Deuteronomy 31:8, Revelation 21:4

[xi] Ann Voskamp is found at www.AHolyExperience.com. Quote used with her gracious permission.

www.ingramcontent.com/pod-product-compliance
Lightning Source LLC
Chambersburg PA
CBHW060533030426
42337CB00021B/4248